A delicious recipes cookbook for everyone is a culinary treasure trove that is filled with mouth-watering recipes that are sure to satisfy any palate. This type of cookbook features a wide variety of recipes, ranging from classic comfort food to modern gourmet creations, making it the perfect choice for anyone who loves to cook and eat.

Each recipe in a delicious recipes cookbook for everyone is carefully crafted to maximize flavor and texture, with a focus on using fresh, high-quality ingredients. The recipes are often accompanied by mouth-watering photographs that showcase the finished dish and inspire readers to get into the kitchen and start cooking.

Some of the most popular recipes in this type of cookbook include savory soups, hearty stews, succulent roasts, zesty pastas, and sweet desserts like cakes and pies. The recipes often include helpful tips and tricks from experienced chefs, which can help readers learn new techniques and improve their cooking skills.

In addition to the recipes, a delicious recipes cookbook for everyone may also include helpful information on food and wine pairing, menu planning, and entertaining tips. This type of cookbook is the perfect resource for anyone looking to host a dinner party, prepare a romantic meal, or simply expand their culinary horizons.

Overall, a delicious recipes cookbook for everyone is an essential addition to any cookbook collection. With its diverse range of recipes and expert guidance, this type of cookbook can provide endless hours of inspiration and culinary enjoyment for home cooks of all levels.

Fish And Chips

Ingredients

900 g potatoes.
sunflower oil , for deep-frying.
225 g white fish fillets , skin off, pin-boned, from sustainable sources.
225 g plain flour , plus extra for dusting.
285 ml cold beer.
3 heaped teaspoons baking powder.
MUSHY PEAS.
a few sprigs of fresh mint.

Fish and chips is a classic dish that's loved by many! With just a few simple ingredients, you can easily make this healthy and easy dinner for kids. Here's how to get it done:

1. Start off by preheating the oven to 190°C/375°F/gas 5. Peel the potatoes, then cut into thick chips. Parboil the chips in boiling salted water for 5-7 minutes, depending on how thick they are. Drain and leave to steam dry while you prepare the fish and batter.

2. Put the flour, baking powder and beer in a large bowl and whisk together until smooth. Dust the fish fillets with a little extra flour, then dip in the batter to coat.

3. Heat the oil in a deep-fat fryer or large saucepan until it reaches 180°C/350°F on a cooking thermometer. Carefully place the chips into the hot fat and fry for 10 minutes or until golden. Drain well on kitchen paper.

4. Reheat the oil until it reaches 190°C/375°F on a cooking thermometer, then deep-fry the fish in batches for 5 minutes or until cooked through and golden. Drain well on kitchen paper and season with salt while still hot.

5. Place the chips onto a baking tray, then cook for 15-20 minutes in the preheated oven until crisp. Serve with the fish and mushy peas, and garnish with fresh mint leaves if desired. Enjoy!

Fish and chips is a great dish to make at home, offering delicious flavors and a healthy dinner option for the whole family. With just a few ingredients, it's easy to whip up in no time. Enjoy!

Chicken Tortellini

Ingredients

2 tablespoons olive oil.
8 oz boneless skinless chicken breast, cut into 1/4-inch slices.
3 cups fresh small broccoli florets.
2 teaspoons chopped garlic.
1 1/2 cups Progresso™ chicken broth (from 32-oz carton)
2 packages (9 oz each) refrigerated cheese tortellini.
1 cup milk.

Preparing a healthy and easy dinner for the kids doesn't have to be a hassle. This delicious Chicken Tortellini is sure to please everyone at the table.

To make this dish, start by heating two tablespoons of olive oil in a large skillet over medium-high heat. Once it's hot, add the chicken slices and cook for about 4 minutes until they're no longer pink. Add the broccoli florets, garlic, and a pinch of salt, then cook for another 3 to 4 minutes.

Next, pour in the Progresso™ chicken broth and bring it to a boil over high heat. Once boiling, add the tortellini and cook for about 8 minutes until the pasta is cooked through. Then, reduce the heat to low and stir in the milk. Simmer for a few more minutes until it thickens up a bit. Taste and season with salt and pepper if needed.

Serve the tortellini with some extra grated Parmesan cheese on top. Enjoy! This Chicken Tortellini is a healthy and delicious dinner that your kids are sure to love. It's quick and easy, ready in just 30 minutes. Enjoy!

*Note: You can customize this dish with other vegetables like mushrooms, bell peppers or spinach. For added protein, you can also add shrimp or cooked sausage. Enjoy!

Enjoy! With its delicious flavor and simple preparation, this Chicken Tortellini is a surefire winner for any family dinner. It's the perfect healthy and easy dinner for kids - ready in just 30 minutes! Bon appetit!

Lasagna

This vegetarian lasagna is a healthy and delicious meal that kids of all ages will enjoy! It's packed with nutritious vegetables, savory tomato sauce, and creamy white sauce. To make this dish, start by preheating your oven to 180°C/Gas Mark 4.

Next, prepare the vegetables: cut the red peppers into large chunks and slice the aubergines into ½ cm thick slices. Heat 8 tablespoons of olive oil in a large frying pan over medium heat and add the red pepper chunks and aubergine slices. Cook for 8-10 minutes until they are lightly browned.

In another pan, add 1 tablespoon of olive oil over medium heat and sauté the onions and garlic until soft. Add the carrot and tomato purée and cook for a few minutes. Pour in the wine and allow it to reduce by half before adding the canned tomatoes. Simmer for 20 minutes until you have a thick sauce. Finally, add the basil leaves and season with salt and pepper.

To make the white sauce, melt the butter in a pan over low heat. Add the flour and stir together until there are no lumps. Gradually add in the milk, stirring constantly until it forms a smooth sauce.

Now you're ready to assemble your vegetarian lasagna! Grease an oven-proof dish with olive oil and begin layering with lasagne sheets, vegetables, tomato sauce, white sauce, mozzarella cheese, and cherry tomatoes. Repeat until you have used all the ingredients and top with extra mozzarella cheese. Bake in the preheated oven for 30 minutes, or until golden brown on top.

This vegetarian lasagna is an easy-to-make dish that kids will love! The vegetables are full of healthy vitamins and minerals, while the tomato and white sauces add a wonderful depth of flavor. Serve it up with a side salad for a complete vegetarian meal that's sure to satisfy even the pickiest eaters. Bon appétit!

Fettuccine Alfredo

Ingredients

1 pound fettuccine noodles (use gluten-free, legume, or zucchini noodles if desired)
4 garlic cloves.
1 small head cauliflower (1 1/2 to 2 pounds), enough for 6 cups florets.
4 tablespoons olive oil.
1 cup raw unsalted cashews.
2 cups vegetable broth.
⅛ teaspoon onion powder.
1/8 + ¼ teaspoon ground black pepper.

ettuccine Alfredo is a healthy pasta dish that you can easily prepare in the comfort of your own home. To make this healthy version, start by boiling the fettuccine noodles according to package instructions. Meanwhile, mince the garlic cloves and cut the head of cauliflower into florets. Heat olive oil in a pan and add the garlic and cauliflower florets. Cook until the cauliflower is tender, stirring occasionally. In a high-speed blender, add the cashews, vegetable broth, onion powder, and black pepper and blend on high speed until smooth. Pour the sauce over the cooked fettuccine noodles and mix to combine. Serve warm and enjoy! With this healthy pasta dish, you can have a delicious meal that's sure to please. Bon Appetit!

Tuna Rice Salad

Ingredients

400g of cold cooked rice.
200g of tinned tuna.
100g of sugar snap peas, halved.
1 red pepper, diced.
2 tomatoes, chopped into small chunks.
3 spring onions, finely sliced.
2 tablespoons of light mayonnaise.
Juice ½ lemon.

This Tuna Rice Salad is an easy and healthy lunch option for kids. It's a tasty combination of flavors that will be sure to please even the pickiest of eaters.

To make this delicious dish, begin by combining 400 grams of cold cooked rice, 200 grams of tinned tuna, 100 grams of sugar snap peas (halved), 1 red pepper (diced), 2 tomatoes (chopped into small chunks) and 3 spring onions (finely sliced). Drizzle with two tablespoons of light mayonnaise and squeeze ½ lemon for a zesty flavor. Mix everything together until all ingredients are well combined.

Serve this Tuna Rice Salad immediately or store it in an airtight container for up to two days. It's a perfect meal for lunch or dinner and can be enjoyed by the whole family.

Enjoy!

Veggie Burritos

Preparing this vegetarian burrito recipe for kids is easy! Start by cooking the cilantro-lime rice according to package instructions. Meanwhile, heat a large skillet over medium-high heat and add oil. When hot, add black beans that have been seasoned with chipotle spice. Cook until heated through and beginning to char, stirring occasionally. Next, add peppers and onions to the pan and cook until softened, about 5 minutes more.

To make the avocado cream sauce, prepare it in a food processor by adding avocado, cilantro, jalapeño, garlic, lime juice and either sour cream or Greek yogurt. Process until fully combined before removing from heat and stirring in 3 Tbsp of water for desired consistency.

Once all components of the vegetarian burrito are ready, have kids help assemble their creation. This recipe is great for vegetarian recipes for kids and healthy recipes they can create themselves! Enjoy!

Pumpkin Pie

INGREDIENTS

1 (15-OUNCE) CAN PUMPKIN PUREE.
1 (12-OUNCE) CAN EVAPORATED MILK.
3 LARGE EGGS.
3/4 CUP GRANULATED ARTIFICIAL SWEETENER, SUCH AS SPLENDA OR TRUVIA.
1 TEASPOON GROUND CINNAMON.
1/2 TEASPOON GROUND GINGER.
1/4 TEASPOON GROUND NUTMEG.
1/4 TEASPOON SALT.

Pumpkin pie is a classic no sugar dessert recipe that can be enjoyed any time of the year. It's a healthy alternative to other high-sugar desserts, and it won't break the calorie bank. Preparing a pumpkin pie is easy with just a few simple steps.

First, preheat your oven to 350°F and grease a 9-inch pie pan.

In a large bowl, mix together 1 (15-ounce) can of pumpkin puree, 1 (12-ounce) can evaporated milk, 3 large eggs, 3/4 cup granulated artificial sweetener such as Splenda or Truvia, 1 teaspoon ground cinnamon, 1/2 teaspoon ground ginger, 1/4 teaspoon ground nutmeg, and 1/4 teaspoon salt. Whisk everything together until combined.

Pour the mixture into the prepared pie pan and bake for 50-55 minutes or until a knife inserted into the center of the pie comes out clean. Let cool before serving. Enjoy!

Bolognese Spaghetti

Ingredients
1 tbsp olive oil.
4 rashers smoked streaky bacon, finely chopped.
2 medium onions, finely chopped.
2 carrots, trimmed and finely chopped.
2 celery sticks, finely chopped.
2 garlic cloves finely chopped.
2-3 sprigs rosemary leaves picked and finely chopped.
500g beef mince.

If you're looking for delicious recipes for kids, look no further than bolognese spaghetti! This classic Italian pasta dish is packed with flavour and can be made in no time. Plus, children of all ages will love it! Here's how to cook the perfect bolognese spaghetti:

Begin by heating 1 tablespoon of olive oil in a large frying pan. Add 4 finely chopped rashers of smoked streaky bacon, 2 finely chopped onions, 2 trimmed and finely chopped carrots, 2 finely chopped celery sticks, 2 finely chopped garlic cloves and the leaves from 2-3 sprigs of rosemary that have been picked and finely chopped. Cook the ingredients until the bacon and vegetables are softened.

Next, add 500g of beef mince to the pan and season with salt and pepper. Stir everything together and cook for about 10 minutes until the mince is browned. Finally, pour in a jar or can of tomato sauce or passata, along with a little water if necessary. Simmer for 10 minutes, then serve over cooked hot spaghetti.

Your delicious bolognese spaghetti dish is now ready to be enjoyed. Add a sprinkle of grated cheese and a dash of chilli flakes if desired. Bon appétit!

Ginger Sesame Noodles

Ginger sesame noodles is an easy vegetarian recipe that's perfect for kids. It's packed with flavor and is a healthy alternative to take-out noodles. To make this delicious dish, you will need 1/2 cup plus 2 tablespoons of low sodium soy sauce or tamari, 1/4 cup honey, 2 tablespoons balsamic vinegar, 2 tablespoons rice vinegar, 3 tablespoons creamy peanut butter or tahini, 1 tablespoon molasses or pomegranate molasses (optional), 2 tablespoons fresh grated ginger and 3 cloves garlic grated.

To begin preparing your ginger sesame noodles dish for your family dinner table, start by mixing together all the ingredients in a bowl until fully combined. Then pour the mixture into a pot, and heat until it comes to a boil. Reduce the heat and simmer for 10 minutes. Once cooked, transfer the noodles into a serving bowl and serve with your favorite vegetarian toppings such as diced tomatoes or avocado slices. Enjoy this vegetarian recipe that's perfect for kids!

Ginger sesame noodles is not only delicious but also healthy and easy to prepare. With the combination of fresh ingredients like honey, ginger and garlic, you can make sure that your family will be enjoying an irresistible meal in no time! Give this vegetarian recipe for kids a try and watch them finish their plates in seconds!

Coconut Yogurt Cake

Ingredients:

2 eggs
¾ cup (180ml) light-flavoured extra virgin olive oil
1 cup (280g) natural Greek-style (thick) yoghurt
2 tablespoons lemon juice
½ cup (110g) caster (superfine) sugar
½ cup (180g) honey
1 cup (80g) desiccated coconut
1¾ cups (225g) white spelt flour
1 teaspoon baking powder
½ teaspoon baking soda
½ teaspoon salt

Instructions:

Preheat the oven to 160°C/320°F.

Grease and line a 22cm round cake tin.

In a large mixing bowl, beat the eggs until light and fluffy.

Add the olive oil, yoghurt, lemon juice, caster sugar, and honey to the bowl, and whisk until well combined.

Fold in the desiccated coconut.

In a separate bowl, sift the spelt flour, baking powder, baking soda, and salt.

Gradually fold the flour mixture into the egg mixture until just combined.

Pour the mixture into the prepared cake tin and smooth the surface with a spatula.

Bake in the preheated oven for 50-60 minutes, or until a skewer inserted into the center of the cake comes out clean.

Remove the cake from the oven and allow it to cool in the tin for 10 minutes.

Turn the cake out onto a wire rack and allow it to cool completely.

Serve the coconut yoghurt cake with a dollop of Greek yoghurt and fresh berries on top.

Enjoy your delicious Coconut Yoghurt Cake!

Vegan Caprese Pasta

INGREDIENTS

12 OUNCES SPAGHETTI (GF IF PREFERRED)
2 TABLESPOONS OLIVE OIL , EXTRA VIRGIN.
¼ TEASPOON CRUSHED RED PEPPER FLAKES (OPTIONAL)
3 CLOVES GARLIC , MINCED.
2 PINTS CHERRY TOMATOES , HALVED.
1 TEASPOON SEA SALT , MORE TO TASTE (OR PREFERRED SALT)
FRESH CRACKED PEPPER , TO TASTE.

This vegetarian vegan caprese pasta is a great meal for kids of all ages. It's healthy and easy to prepare, so even the youngest chefs can help out! To make this delicious vegetarian recipe, start by bringing a pot of salted water to boil. Once boiling, add the spaghetti and cook according to package instructions until al dente.

While the spaghetti cooks, heat olive oil in a large skillet over medium-high heat. Add crushed red pepper flakes (if desired) garlic, cherry tomatoes, salt and pepper; stir frequently until vegetables are tender and fragrant.

Once the spaghetti is cooked, drain it and place it back into the pot; top with prepared vegetables and combine gently. Serve hot or chilled, with freshly grated Parmesan cheese if desired. Enjoy!

This vegetarian vegan caprese pasta is a great option for anyone looking to add a healthy and delicious meal to their weekly menu. It's also vegetarian, making it perfect for kids who are vegetarian or transitioning towards vegetarianism. With just a few ingredients and some basic cooking techniques, you can have this tasty dish ready in no time! So give it a try today and see how much your family loves it!

Shrimp Pasta

Ingredients

8 ounces fettuccine.
1 pound medium shrimp, peeled and deveined.
Kosher salt and freshly ground black pepper, to taste.
8 tablespoons 1 stick unsalted butter, divided.
4 cloves garlic, minced.
½ teaspoon dried oregano.
½ teaspoon crushed red pepper flakes.
2 cups baby arugula.

Shrimp Pasta is a healthy and easy dinner for kids that you can whip up in no time. To prepare it, start by bringing a large pot of salted water to a boil over high heat. Once boiling, add the fettuccine and cook until al dente according to package directions. Drain pasta into a colander and set aside.

Meanwhile, in a large skillet over medium heat, melt 4 tablespoons of butter. Add the shrimp and season with salt and pepper to taste. Cook, stirring occasionally until pink and cooked through, about 3-4 minutes; set aside.

To the same skillet add remaining butter, garlic, oregano and red pepper flakes. Cook, stirring frequently, until fragrant, about 1-2 minutes. Stir in the cooked pasta and shrimp; season with salt and pepper to taste.

Finally, stir in the arugula until wilted, about 1 minute. Serve immediately, garnished with more red pepper flakes if desired. Enjoy!

Crispy Black Bean And Sweet Potato Tacos

Ingredients
8-10 tortillas (see notes)
2 14 oz can black beans, drained.
2 sweet potatoes, diced (skin on or peeled)
1 Tablespoon oil.
1/2 teaspoon (each) cumin, paprika, chili powder.
1/2 teaspoon garlic powder.
salt to taste.

These vegetarian black bean and sweet potato tacos are an easy, healthy, and delicious way to get your kids eating vegetarian! They can be made in under 30 minutes with very few ingredients - perfect for busy nights. To prepare, simply heat up the oil in a large skillet over medium-high heat. Add in the diced sweet potatoes and season with cumin, paprika, chili powder, garlic powder and salt. Cook until the potatoes are soft (about 10 minutes). Then add in the drained black beans and cook for another 2-3 minutes until everything is heated through.

To assemble the tacos grab 8-10 tortillas (or however many you like) spread some of the mixture on each taco shell then top with your favorite toppings like shredded cheese, tomatoes, lettuce, or salsa. Enjoy!

These vegetarian tacos are a great way to get your kids eating healthier and trying new vegetarian recipes. They're easy to make, full of flavor, and customizable with whatever toppings you have on hand. Give these vegetarian black bean and sweet potato tacos a try for your next vegetarian dinner! Your family will love them.

Strawberry Toast

Strawberry Toast is a healthy and tasty breakfast option for kids that's easy to prepare. To make it, start by melting the butter in a medium-sized skillet over medium heat. Add the sliced strawberries and cook for 5 minutes or until the berries have softened. Next, add the maple syrup, orange zest, non-fat milk, and teaspoon of salt. Cook for another 3 minutes or until the mixture thickens. Finally, place the slices of cinnamon raisin bread in a single layer on top of the strawberry mixture. Crack three eggs over the toast and let cook until the whites are set and yolks have just started to become soft. Serve immediately with a sprinkle of extra orange zest. Enjoy!

Cheese Pizza

Are you craving delicious pizza but don't know how to prepare one? Look no further, as we have the perfect cheese pizza recipe for you! To make this delicious meal, you will need 1/2 recipe of homemade pizza crust, 1/2-3/4 cup (127-190g) of your favorite pizza sauce (homemade or store-bought), 8 ounces of sliced mozzarella cheese, 1 and 1/2 cups (6oz or 168g) shredded mozzarella cheese, 2-3 Tablespoons (10-15g) grated Parmesan cheese, and dried basil or Italian seasoning.

To begin, preheat your oven to 425°F (218°C). Then spread out the pizza dough on a baking sheet or pizza pan. Next, spread the sauce over the pizza crust, then top with sliced and shredded mozzarella cheese. Sprinkle parmesan cheese and dried basil/Italian seasoning over the top of the pizza. Bake for 12-15 minutes until the cheese is melted and golden brown. Let cool slightly before cutting into slices to serve. Enjoy your delicious homemade cheese pizza!

With a few simple ingredients, you can enjoy delicious homemade cheese pizza in no time! So what are you waiting for? Try out this delicious recipe today!

Spinach & Tuna Pancakes

Ingredients

2 tsp rapeseed oil.
2 garlic cloves, chopped.
250g baby spinach.
1 tbsp tomato purée.
120g can tuna steak in spring water, drained.
200g cottage cheese.
2 large eggs.
4 tbsp plain wholemeal flour.

These delicious spinach and tuna pancakes are simple to make and packed with flavour. A great way to get kids eating their vegetables!

To make these healthy lunch recipes for kids, you will need: 2 tsp rapeseed oil, 2 garlic cloves chopped, 250g baby spinach, 1 tbsp tomato purée, 120g can tuna steak in spring water, drained, 200g cottage cheese, 2 large eggs and 4 tbsp plain wholemeal flour.

First heat the oil in a medium-sized pan set over a low heat. Add the garlic and cook for 1 minute until lightly golden; then add the spinach and tomato purée and cook, stirring often, for 3 minutes until the spinach has wilted. Add the tuna and cottage cheese to the pan and stir everything together; then season with some salt and pepper.

In a separate bowl, whisk together the eggs and flour until smooth. Pour this over the ingredients in the pan, stirring them together carefully with a wooden spoon. When everything is combined, turn up the heat to medium and cook, stirring occasionally, until the mixture thickens slightly.

Divide the pancakes into 4-5 portions and spoon into a plate. Serve with a salad or vegetables of your choice for an easy and healthy lunch recipe that kids will love! Enjoy!

Pan Pizza

Making delicious pan pizza is easier than you think with the right ingredients. To make your own delicious pan pizza, start by combining 2 1/4 cups of all-purpose flour and 1 teaspoon of kosher salt in a large bowl. Sprinkle in 3/4 teaspoon of active dry yeast, then add 3/4 cup plus 3 tablespoons of lukewarm water and mix until the dough comes together. Knead the dough on a lightly floured surface for about 5 minutes until it is smooth and elastic. Transfer the dough to an oiled bowl, cover with plastic wrap, and let rise for at least one hour.

Meanwhile, prepare the toppings by mashing two cloves of garlic with one tablespoon olive oil until it forms a paste. Spread one tablespoon of olive oil over the bottom of a greased 10-inch skillet, then roll out the dough in the pan until it covers the base. Spread the garlic paste and tomato sauce over the dough, sprinkle with some dried oregano, and bake for 18 to 20 minutes at 400°F. Enjoy your delicious pizza hot from the oven!

Making delicious pan pizza does not have to be complicated - all you need is some simple ingredients and a few steps to get started. With just a little patience and practice, you can create delicious pizzas that will impress anyone! Try experimenting with different toppings or flavor combinations to make new delicious recipes each time. So what are you waiting for? Get making delicious pizza in no time!

Happy cooking!

Crispy Potato Tacos

INGREDIENTS

2 LARGE RUSSET POTATOES.
¾ CUP SOUR CREAM.
2 CLOVES GARLIC, MINCED.
½ TEASPOON CUMIN.
SALT, TO TASTE.
½ TEASPOON OREGANO.
8 CORN TORTILLAS.
OIL, FOR FRYING.

Crispy potato tacos are a healthy vegetarian recipe for kids that is easy to prepare. Start by preheating your oven to 400°F and scrubbing the potatoes clean. Cut them into thin slices, about ¼-inch thick, and place onto a baking sheet lined with parchment paper. Drizzle with oil and sprinkle with salt, then bake for 25 minutes or until golden brown.

While the potatoes are baking, make the sour cream garlic sauce by combining the sour cream, minced garlic, cumin, oregano and salt in a bowl. Mix ingredients until everything is well combined.

Once the potatoes have finished baking, heat up some oil in a large skillet over high heat. Place four of the tortillas in the skillet and cook for 30-45 seconds per side until lightly browned. Place them on a plate lined with paper towels to absorb any excess oil.

To assemble tacos, place two potato slices inside each tortilla, then top with some of the sour cream garlic sauce and fold in half. Repeat this process with the remaining four tortillas and serve immediately. Enjoy!

These vegetarian crispy potato tacos are sure to be a hit amongst kids and adults alike! So next time you're looking for an easy, healthy vegetarian recipe for kids, try making these delicious tacos. They'll definitely make dinner time much more fun!

Banana Chia Pudding

INGREDIENTS

2 LARGE OVERRIPE BANANAS.
2 CUPS UNSWEETENED COCONUT (BEVERAGE), ALMOND OR CASHEW MILK.
6 TABLESPOONS CHIA SEEDS.

Banana Chia Pudding is a no sugar dessert recipe that anyone can prepare in no time at all! It's healthy and delicious, making it the perfect treat for any occasion. To make this tasty no-sugar dessert, you'll need two overripe bananas, two cups of unsweetened coconut (beverage), almond or cashew milk, and six tablespoons of chia seeds. First, mash the bananas in a bowl until no lumps remain. Add the milk and stir to combine. Then add the chia seeds and stir again until everything is mixed together well. Cover the bowl with plastic wrap and place it in the refrigerator for a few hours or overnight. Once the chia pudding has thickened and all of the ingredients have blended together, you can enjoy it! Serve it with fresh fruit or your favorite topping. Banana Chia Pudding is a no sugar dessert recipe that's sure to satisfy any sweet tooth! Enjoy!

Strawberry and Rhubarb Cobbler

Ingredients

4 cups (567g) rhubarb, diced.
1 quart (567g) strawberries, washed and sliced, or thawed if frozen.
1 cup (198g) granulated sugar.
3 tablespoons (32g) quick-cooking tapioca or 3 tablespoons (21g) cornstarch

For the fruit filling:

Preheat the oven to 375°F (190°C).
In a large bowl, combine the diced rhubarb, sliced strawberries, granulated sugar, and tapioca or cornstarch. Mix well and let the mixture sit for about 15 minutes, stirring occasionally, until the fruit has released some of its juices and the sugar and tapioca have formed a syrup.

For the cobbler topping:

In a separate large bowl, whisk together the flour, sugar, baking powder, and salt. Add the cold butter and use a pastry blender or your fingers to cut it into the flour mixture until it resembles coarse crumbs.
Add the milk and stir until a soft dough forms. It's okay if it's a bit lumpy.

To assemble and bake:

Transfer the fruit filling to a 9x13-inch (23x33-cm) baking dish or a similar-sized dish. Dollop the cobbler dough on top of the fruit in spoonfuls, leaving some gaps so the fruit can peek through.
Bake for 40-50 minutes, or until the cobbler topping is golden brown and the fruit filling is bubbling and thickened.
Remove from the oven and let cool for a few minutes before serving. Top with whipped cream or ice cream, if desired. Enjoy your delicious Strawberry and Rhubarb Cobbler!

Salmon And Cream Cheese Sandwich

Ingredients
Bread. ...
Whipped Cream Cheese. ...
Smoked Salmon. ...
Fresh Chives. ...
Fresh Parsley. ...
Salt and Black Pepper.

This easy-to-make sandwich is a great way to introduce kids to the delicious flavors of smoked salmon! Start by taking two slices of whole wheat bread and spreading a generous layer of whipped cream cheese on one side. Layer on some thinly sliced smoked salmon, and top with fresh chives, parsley, salt and black pepper for flavor. Serve up with a side of fruit for a healthy, delicious and fun lunch that the kids will love! Enjoy!

No Egg Pancakes

Making vegetarian-friendly no egg pancakes is a quick, easy and healthy way to appeal to your kids' taste buds. This recipe can be easily adapted for vegetarian diets and there are only a few simple ingredients needed to make it. Here's how you can prepare vegetarian no egg pancakes in just a few minutes:

Ingredients:
- 1 1/4 cups all-purpose flour
- 1 tablespoon baking powder
- 1 tablespoon sugar
- 1/4 teaspoon salt
- 1 cup non-fat or 1% milk
- 2 tablespoons vegetable oil
- 2 tablespoons water

Instructions:
1. In a large bowl, combine the flour, baking powder, sugar and salt.

2. In a separate bowl, mix together the milk, vegetable oil and water until it forms a thick paste.

3. Slowly pour the liquid ingredients into the dry ones while mixing with a whisk or fork until you have a batter without any lumps.

4. Heat a non-stick pan over medium heat and grease it lightly with vegetable oil.

5. Drop one tablespoon of the batter into the center of the pan at a time and spread it evenly to form small pancakes. Cook each side for about 1-2 minutes or until golden brown.

6. Serve vegetarian no egg pancakes with your favorite toppings such as butter, honey or syrup.

Making vegetarian no egg pancakes is an easy way to add a healthy and delicious meal to your child's diet. It's sure to be a hit with the whole family! Enjoy!

Egg On Avocado Toast

Avocado toast is a delicious, vegetarian-friendly and healthy meal for kids. Preparing it is simple and doesn't require many ingredients. Here's how you can make an egg on avocado toast recipe:

To start, you'll need one slice of whole grain or gluten-free bread that has been toasted. I recommend Dave's Killer Bread Good Seed Thin Sliced for the perfect texture and flavor. After toasting, spread a thin layer of mashed avocado (about one ounce from a quarter of a small haas avocado) onto the bread.

Next, spray cooking oil into a pan and crack an egg in the center. Cook until the egg whites are set and the yolk is still runny. Season with salt and pepper to taste, then carefully slide onto the avocado toast.

Optionally, you can add a few hot sauce or red pepper flakes for an extra kick of flavor. Serve immediately and enjoy this vegetarian-friendly egg on avocado toast recipe!

Kids will love this delicious, healthy and vegetarian-friendly meal. With a few simple steps, they can enjoy this tasty breakfast or lunch with minimal effort. Egg on avocado toast is the perfect dish for busy mornings and afternoons!

Happy cooking!

Chocolate Bread And Butter Pudding

Ingredients

40g unsalted butter, softened, plus extra for greasing the tin.
8 slices white bread, cut into medium slices (preferably 1 day old)
50g raisins & cranberries mix.
400ml whole milk.
50ml double cream.
1 x 100g bar dark chocolate (70% cocoa solids), roughly chopped.
75g caster sugar.
1 orange, zested.

Here are the instructions for making chocolate bread and butter pudding:

Preheat the oven to 180°C (160°C fan)/350°F/gas mark 4. Grease a 1.5-litre ovenproof dish with butter.

Spread the softened butter on one side of each slice of bread, then cut them into quarters.

Arrange half of the bread slices, buttered-side up, in the bottom of the prepared dish. Sprinkle half of the raisins and cranberries over the bread.

In a saucepan, gently heat the milk, cream, chocolate, sugar, and orange zest, stirring constantly until the chocolate has melted and the sugar has dissolved.

In a separate bowl, beat the eggs together. Pour the chocolate mixture over the eggs, whisking continuously.

Pour half of the chocolate custard mixture over the bread in the dish, then add the remaining bread slices, buttered-side up, and sprinkle over the remaining raisins and cranberries. Pour the remaining chocolate custard over the top.

Let the pudding sit for 15-20 minutes, so the bread absorbs some of the custard.

Place the dish in a roasting tin, then fill the tin with hot water until it comes halfway up the sides of the pudding dish.

Bake the pudding for 35-40 minutes or until it is set and the bread is golden brown.

Serve the bread and butter pudding warm with a dollop of whipped cream, if desired.

Basil Pizza

Ingredients

1 recipe Pizza Dough, stretched onto a 14-inch pizza pan or large baking sheet.
½ heaping cup Pizza Sauce.
8 ounces fresh mozzarella cheese, torn or sliced.
½ cup thinly sliced cherry tomatoes.
10 fresh basil leaves.
Pinch red pepper flakes.
Extra-virgin olive oil, for drizzling.

This delicious homemade basil pizza is sure to be a hit with your family and friends. Start by preheating the oven to 450°F (232°C). Then, stretch out one recipe of Pizza Dough onto a 14-inch pizza pan or large baking sheet. Spread ½ heaping cup of Pizza Sauce over the dough, followed by 8 ounces of torn or sliced fresh mozzarella cheese, ½ cup thinly sliced cherry tomatoes, 10 fresh basil leaves, and a pinch of red pepper flakes. Drizzle lightly with extra-virgin olive oil before baking in the preheated oven for 17-20 minutes until golden brown. Serve hot as an appetizer or main course! This delicious basil pizza recipe is sure to become one of your go-to delicious pizza recipes. Enjoy!

Vegetarian Egg Muffins

Vegetarian egg muffins are a great way to get your kids excited about vegetarian recipes. Not only are they healthy and delicious, but they're so easy to prepare! All you need is a few simple ingredients, some basic kitchen tools, and you can have vegetarian egg muffins ready in no time. To begin, gather the ingredients - 3 cups of mixed vegetables (such as broccoli, mushrooms, peppers, and spinach), 1 teaspoon oil, 12 large eggs, ¼ cup milk, ½ teaspoon black pepper & salt to taste, ½ teaspoon dry mustard powder, 3 tablespoons onion minced and 1 cup cheddar cheese.

In a large bowl whisk together the eggs with the milk until well combined. Add the seasonings with the oil and then add in the vegetables, onion, and cheese. Mix everything together until all ingredients are evenly distributed.

Using a muffin tin lined with paper liners or sprayed with non-stick cooking spray, evenly spoon the vegetarian egg mixture into each cup. Bake in preheated oven for about 20 minutes, or until egg muffins are cooked through.

Once cooked, vegetarian egg muffins can be served warm or cold and make excellent snacks for kids. They are a great grab-and-go option for lunchboxes and after school snacks that your kids will love! With just a few simple ingredients and minimal preparation, vegetarian egg muffins are a healthy and delicious option for kids. Try them today and let your kids enjoy the vegetarian recipes!

Strawberry Quinoa Smoothie

This smoothie recipe is perfect for kids and health-conscious adults alike. It's packed with superfoods like quinoa, chia seeds, and wheat germ to give your smoothie a nutrient boost. Here's how to prepare it:

First, gather all the necessary ingredients – 1 large ripe banana, 1 (6 oz) low-fat vanilla Greek yogurt, 1/2 cup cooked quinoa (cooled), 2 Tablespoons honey, 1 Tablespoon chia seeds, 1 Tablespoon wheat germ, 2 cups frozen strawberries (if using fresh, freeze them first), and 1-1/2 cups vanilla almond milk.

Next, add the banana, yogurt, honey, chia seeds, wheat germ and almond milk to a blender. Blend until smooth.

Finally, add the quinoa and frozen strawberries to the smoothie and blend again until smooth. Pour into glasses and enjoy!

This delicious smoothie is healthy, tasty and easy to make – perfect for kids or as a healthy snack for adults. Enjoy!

Vegan Mashed Potatoes

Vegan mashed potatoes are a delicious and healthy vegetarian recipe that's perfect for kids. With this simple recipe, you can easily prepare vegan mashed potatoes that your family is sure to love!

To get started, simply wash and scrub 6-8 medium yukon gold potatoes (if large, cut in half) and add them to a pot. Cover the potatoes with water, add 1/2 tsp of sea salt, and bring to a boil. Boil the potatoes until they are tender, about 15-20 minutes.

Once the potatoes are cooked, drain them and mash them using your favorite method. We prefer a potato masher or an electric mixer for best results. Once mashed, add 1/2 tsp of ground black pepper and 5-6 cloves of raw or roasted garlic (or sub minced garlic sautéed for 3 minutes in olive oil). Gently mix the ingredients until fully incorporated and then add 3-4 tablespoons of vegan butter (such as Earth Balance) to give it a creamy texture.

Season to taste, and you're done! Serve your vegan mashed potatoes hot with a sprinkle of salt and pepper. Your family will love this vegetarian recipe that's both healthy and delicious! Enjoy!

Goat Cheese Pizza

Goat Cheese Pizza is a delicious recipe that is both easy to make and delicious to eat. This delicious pizza combines delicious ingredients like homemade pizza sauce, mozzarella cheese, soft goat cheese, red onion slices and oregano into a delicious combination that will have your family coming back for seconds!

To start off this delicious meal, you will need one recipe of either the Best Pizza Dough, Thin Crust Pizza Dough or Pizza Oven Dough. Once you have the dough prepared, spread ⅓ cup of Homemade Pizza Sauce on top. Then sprinkle ½ cup of shredded mozzarella cheese over top. Break up 3 ounces of soft goat cheese (chevre) and dot it around the pizza. Lastly add 1 handful of red onion slices and a sprinkle of ¼ teaspoon dried oregano. Finish off the pizza by adding some kosher salt and fresh ground black pepper to taste.

Once all your delicious ingredients are added, bake in an oven preheated to 500°F for 10-15 minutes or until the cheese is melted and bubbly. For a delicious finishing touch, garnish with some fresh basil leaves before serving.

Try this delicious Goat Cheese Pizza recipe tonight and enjoy delicious, easy-to-make pizza that's sure to be a hit! Enjoy!

Focaccia Pizza

If you're looking for delicious pizza recipes, then look no further than focaccia pizza! This popular Italian dish is simple to prepare and full of delicious tastes. To get started, you'll need the following ingredients: 3 cups (15oz/422g) all-purpose flour, ½ teaspoon instant yeast, 2 teaspoons salt, 1 ⅓ cups (10 ½oz/282ml) water at room temperature, 2 tablespoons olive oil, ½ cup (4oz/115g) pizza sauce, 1 ½ cups (8oz/225g) mozzarella grated, and 10-12 pepperoni slices (optional).

To begin preparing this delicious dish, preheat your oven to 450°F. In a large bowl, mix together the flour, yeast, and salt. Once that's done, add in the water and olive oil and stir until a dough is formed. Knead it for 5 minutes on a lightly floured surface. Grease a 14-inch baking pan with olive oil before transferring your dough to it. Press the dough into the pan using your fingertips to form an even layer. Brush with additional oil if needed, then bake at 450°F for 12 minutes.

Once the crust has cooked through, remove from oven and spread pizza sauce over top followed by mozzarella and pepperoni (if desired). Bake again for 10-15 minutes or until cheese is melted and bubbling. Let cool slightly before cutting into slices and serving. Enjoy your delicious focaccia pizza!

You can also customize this delicious dish by adding any additional toppings of your choice! From mushrooms to bell peppers, the possibilities are endless. Give it a try and let us know how delicious your focaccia pizza turned out! Bon Appétit!

Chocolate Chip Cookies

Making chocolate chip cookies is a fun and easy way to enjoy a no sugar dessert. To begin, preheat your oven to 375°F. Then prepare the ingredients: in a medium bowl, whisk together 2 cups of all-purpose flour, 1 teaspoon of baking soda and ½ teaspoon of salt; set aside. In another large bowl, mix 1 cup of softened butter and the sucralose-granulated sugar blend and sucralose-brown sugar blend together with an electric mixer until they are creamy. After that, add 2 teaspoons of vanilla extract and 2 eggs to the mixture. Beat until everything is combined. Gradually add the flour mixture to the wet ingredients and mix until everything is fully blended.

Finally, fold in your desired amount of chocolate chips into the dough. Drop spoonfuls of dough on an ungreased baking sheet and bake for 10-12 minutes or until golden brown. Let them cool before enjoying this healthy dessert! Enjoy your no sugar cookie masterpiece!

Lemon Tart

Ingredients:

For the pastry crust:

1 1/2 cups all-purpose flour
1/2 cup unsalted butter, chilled and cubed
1/4 cup confectioners' sugar
1 large egg yolk
2 tablespoons ice water

For the lemon filling:

1 tablespoon lemon zest (1 lemon's worth)
1/2 cup lemon juice (from 1 - 2 lemons)
3/4 cup white sugar
12 tablespoons (170g) unsalted butter, cut into 1cm (1/2") cubes
3 whole large eggs
3 large egg yolks

Instructions:

To make the pastry crust, place the flour, butter, and confectioners' sugar in a food processor and pulse until the mixture resembles coarse breadcrumbs. Add the egg yolk and ice water and pulse until the dough comes together.
Turn the dough out onto a lightly floured surface and knead briefly until smooth. Flatten into a disk, wrap in plastic wrap, and refrigerate for 30 minutes.
Preheat the oven to 350°F (180°C).
Roll out the pastry on a lightly floured surface and use to line a 9-inch (23cm) tart tin with a removable bottom. Prick the base with a fork and refrigerate for 15 minutes.
Line the pastry case with baking paper and fill with baking beads or uncooked rice. Bake for 10 minutes, then remove the paper and beads and bake for a further 5 minutes, or until lightly golden.
To make the lemon filling, place the lemon zest, lemon juice, sugar, and butter in a heatproof bowl set over a saucepan of simmering water (making sure the bowl doesn't touch the water). Stir until the butter has melted and the mixture is smooth.
Whisk together the eggs and egg yolks in a separate bowl. Gradually whisk in the lemon mixture.
Pour the lemon filling into the pastry case and bake for 20-25 minutes, or until the filling is just set. Allow to cool to room temperature before serving.
Enjoy your delicious lemon tart!

I want to take a moment to express my heartfelt gratitude for your recent purchase of my recipe book. As a passionate food lover, nothing makes me happier than sharing my favorite recipes with others. Your decision to invest in my book not only supports my dream, but also shows your commitment to expanding your culinary horizons.

I sincerely hope that the recipes in the book will inspire you to try new things and add some excitement to your meals.

Thank you again for your support and for being a part of this journey with me. I hope my book will bring you many happy and delicious moments in the kitchen.

www.ingramcontent.com/pod-product-compliance
Lightning Source LLC
Chambersburg PA
CBHW041150110526
44590CB00027B/4184